The Glory of the Nightingales

THE MACMILLAN COMPANY
NEW YORK · BOSTON · CHICAGO · DALLAS
ATLANTA · SAN FRANCISCO

MACMILLAN & CO., Limited
LONDON · BOMBAY · CALCUTTA
MELBOURNE

THE MACMILLAN COMPANY
OF CANADA, Limited
TORONTO

The Glory of the Nightingales

By

Edwin Arlington Robinson

New York
The Macmillan Company
1930

Reprinted September, 1930.
Reprinted October 1930. Twice.
November, 1930.

TO THE MEMORY OF
ALFRED H. LOUIS

CONTENTS

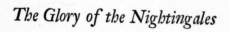

The Glory of the Nightingales

THE GLORY OF THE NIGHTINGALES

I

WITH a long way before him there to Sharon,
    And a longer way from Sharon to the sea,
Alone with an invisible companion
That was a valediction and a vengeance,
There were no further leagues or weary hours
Worth reckoning; for after years of hours,
And hours of years, the way ahead of him
Was like a line drawn surely, to be followed
With no great haste and with no hesitation,
Through time to silence. At the end of time
There would be Nightingale, and his last song—
A noxious and inevitable jest
That like a soft-winged insect at his ear
Fluttered and clung, or flew away from him,
Only to come once more. Weary of that,
And of a sun that burned the firmament,
He rested underneath a wayside oak
That he remembered. He was far from home
Or from a place that once had such a name,
Though not so far now as to be a stranger
To things familiar and so long forgotten
As not to be the same, or quite so large.
The way from here to there was not so long
As in his youth he would have measured it;

The Glory of the Nightingales

The trees and hills and houses that he found
Were not so high; and hours that once had held
So large a rationing of the time of life
Were not so large or long. He might perhaps
Have counted them as longer than they were,
But for a fever in the certainty
Of what he sought. When once he had found that,
And had it, hours might have their way with him,
Or cease. With his work done so righteously,
Dying would not be much to pay for death,
Which was attuned and indispensable
To quivering destiny. No surer part
Was yet assigned to man for a performance
Than one that was for Malory, who must act,
Or leave the stage a failure.

       For the present
All his wealth was in a purpose and a weapon,
All his purpose a removal of one being
Whose inception and existence was an error,
By fate repudiated and presented
To Malory for extinction. Nightingale
Had robbed him long ago of all the rest,
And with a smiling insolence not human
Had watched him crawling maimed out of a wreck
That had been life. There was no life since then;
For man, even if divine, is mechanism
While he is here, and so is not himself

Part First

If much of him be broken. Nightingale
Had shattered Malory, and as autumn waits
Unfailingly for summer to be done,
There was a story waiting to be told
By Malory, who believed he knew the peak
And issue of it—like so many of us
Whose knowing is belief, and whose belief
Is a determination to believe,
Whether in God, or in deflated friends,
Or in ourselves. If we believe enough
In something—none shall tell another what—
That's ours to do, we are glad to be alive,
As Malory was, to do it. For some years
He had closed his eyes at night infallibly
On the same swift and satisfying picture
That in the morning would awaken him
Like a strong voice, or like a strong hand laid
Heavily on him, or like a bell struck once
To make him leap and think, and ask of life
What soiled and veiled necessity of space
Was there somewhere appointed and permitted
For one who must not live. Somewhere alive
He was; and when time whispered where he was,
Malory's part would be to smile and heed
And listen, and to follow and perform.
The larger doings of mortality
Must honor their importance to be done
Becomingly and right, as a seed grows

The Glory of the Nightingales

To a green shoot and so to a round flower.
The fiery-flying stars are in no haste,
And seen from here are still. So Malory's
Undying and unimpeded inspiration
Might have been watched and read by any of us,
As through the immeasurable distances
That are between the nearest and most known
Of loving and unfathomable strangers,
For patience, calm and kind. Patient it was,
As lightning is, or as volcanoes are
That are already alive with fire and death.

Patience under an oak, there by the road
That wound and climbed a silent way to Sharon,
Would then have been about what a wayfarer,
Passing him, might have said was Malory.
If he had paused, and tarried for a while,
He might have found a man somewhat the worse
For wear within, and not unworn without—
One of the passable and unprosperous
To whom life clings; and might have said of him:
"There was a man I found one afternoon
Under an oak. He was a gracious man,
Who must once have had more to do with life
Than he was doing when I found him there.
He was a man of dreams more than of deeds—
Dreams that had not abundantly come true.
Disaster, manifest all over him,

[6]

Part First

Covered and held him like another skin
That was itself another nakedness,
To him, I trust, invisible. His eyes
Were kind, and bright enough; they were almost
Too bright for eyes that were so tired of seeing
No ships come in. For there was fire behind
Their light, and it would be there for some time
Before there was defeat. Meanwhile disaster,
Which is another name for something else,
Sat with him while we talked, under that oak,
And talked with me. Disaster was adept
In courtesy, and as I discovered soon,
In learning beyond mine. His history
He kept untold, more than to tell me once
He was a doctor—which was partly why
He sat in the shade. He smiled, saying that to me,
And saying it, smiled no more. And there I left him,
Alone, to ponder on the Lord knows what."

Could Malory then have heard and seen himself
So passively presented, and in words
That were so near to an obituary,
He might have conjured up another smile
To pay a stranger for his penetration.
Few would have seen so much as that of him,
And fewer, seeing it, would have guessed how little
It was they saw. We should not all sleep well,
If night revealed to us our ignorance

The Glory of the Nightingales

Of others whose intents and evidences,
Errors and excellences, we have assayed
And tabulated. How many a one we meet
Would somewhat rather see us in a coffin,
Is not a thought for any far pursuit
On our part; and of all men, Nightingale
Would have disowned it and forgotten it
As an ingenious waste of meditation
In his impressive mansion by the sea—
A mausoleum that had been his dream
Until he had it. Now he had sea and mansion,
And having them had nothing. He had lost,
Like many in winning, more than he had won;
And he was lonelier there than one man left
On a well-furnished island. Nightingale
Had broken Malory, and was now alone
With his advantages and was believing,
Or saying so to himself, that he had acted
As a man must who is too strong to choose—
A pearl of his invention, therefore lustred
Not like a real one. He had always carried
More of a thwarted vision, and more wisdom,
Lost in himself, than an alluring world
Would let him use; and all being so adjusted,
It was ingratitude for Malory
To meddle with fate in any such thankless way
As his had been; for with his dream of healing,
And his foreshadowed confirmation of it,

Part First

He should have recognized, with no romance
Misleading him, his way that was appointed.
A man by nature dedicated only
To nature's hard submission, should have paid
The price of higher service—failing which,
Now there was nothing of him but a name
Of one forgotten. Where he was not forgotten,
He was among the most of all unenvied
Who have survived their dreams. It was a story
Of a worm boring in a noble tree,
And one there was no need of saying over:
Nature, that made the tree, had made the worm,
And Nightingale was not responsible.

Though his name, as a name treasured, was forgotten,
And his neighborhood was now not anywhere,
Malory felt that home was mocking him
In scenes and silences. He walked along,
Seeing everywhere familiar sights and landmarks,
And everywhere an insolence of change
That almost angered him, until he thought
How far change was from caring what he thought,
Or what he was, or whether he was alive
Or not alive. If there were a few left
To meet with more constraint than interest
An unimportant prodigal returning
In his adversity to the wrong town,
They would ask how he was, and having passed him,

The Glory of the Nightingales

They would look back at him and shake their heads;
They would remember how he had betrayed them,
And hurt their faith. Where friends have sown their faith,
And waited amiably for a late harvest,
Only success deceives; and one man gone
From Sharon would be tragedy as lasting
As one bee missing from a hive, perhaps.

But Malory sought neither faith nor welcome
From one alive, and he had none to give,
Or to inflict, in Sharon, on the living.
He had not come to parley with the living,
And he would not be long there with the dead —
Though she must hear him. She must know at last
That he was doing well, and hear him say so,
And she must give him thanks. Omnipotence
Had erred enough already in fashioning
His best friend as the devil, and would surely
Grant him a word with one the devil had slain
As venomously as any snake in darkness.
There was only Nightingale who came alive
Out of that darkness; therefore she must know
That fate was on its way to Nightingale.
Malory was too patient and sustained
In his malevolence to be mistaken.
He had not come so far to come for nothing,
He had been told the way for him to take.
Assurance, hovering like a benediction,

Had been his one companion. He was right,
Or nothing was right—in which complexity,
All might as well have the same end together.
It was almost a pity that in his arm
There was not power enough to dislocate
Creation. He felt and heard from silent places
A murmur as of all things mocking him
And his assurance as he moved along,
Which may have been a remnant left in him
Of an ancestral fear. He would not ask
Of silence what it was, for while his work
Was there ahead of him, it was not done.
When that was done, there would be nothing left
Worth asking, for the answer would be there;
The seed of a rich purpose would have grown
To the round flower of its accomplishment.

Agatha would be glad when all was over;
For even in that last hillside house of hers,
She must be troubled and humiliated
That he should wait so long, who had not known
At what precarious and intense a temper
The metal of his machinery was made.
Passion for what he sought had worn the face
Of patience, and had fooled him to endure
The wingless crawl of time in his pursuit
And conquest of invisible destroyers;
And when the mask had crumbled, and was gone,

The Glory of the Nightingales

Pursuit had gone mysteriously with it,
So that henceforward there was nothing left
Of Malory but some primitive wheels and springs,
Wound still to go till he was tired of them,
And of their ticking. Now there was no need
Of more oblivion, or excess, or nonsense—
Now that he saw, now that he was awake,
Now that he was alive. He was a king,
Whose word was life or death; and it was death.

II

WITH a wealth beyond a mortal estimation,
    And not heavy, though it had the weight of doom,
He had come from other cities there to Sharon,
Where a woman had been left too long alone.
So it was time for him to think of twilight,
Before there was an end of a long day;
For the sun would soon be drowned in its own fire,
Like a burning ship that, sinking, burns the sea.
Now it was time to find the road below him,
Outside the town—the town he would not enter
Till Agatha had heard him and been happy
To know that ruin for him had not been waste.
Agatha must be told. They would be there
Alone together, and science would have no eye
To censure them. There was no science left
In Sharon since her going away from him
So quietly, so forgetful of what life
Had done; and there was none left anywhere,
While Nightingale was left.

                    With his arms folded,
And his eyes watching long across a valley
More than was there, and across more than valleys,
Malory would have had a brief regard
For any such foreign shaft of observation
As chance or curiosity might have aimed
At him in passing; and he would have felt it

The Glory of the Nightingales

As a post feels a fly. When he had watched
Enough, or seen that watching would reveal
Only what he had found, he moved along,
And soon was on a lower road that led him
Nearer than he could yet believe he was
To one of those three places he had come
So far to find. Two of them were so near
That he could see them, or see where they were,
For it was not a long way now to Sharon;
And even that last of ways would be no longer
Than a way there was from Sharon to the sea.

When he found himself a stranger in the silence
Of a city whose inhabitants were names,
He wandered, pausing, on his way to hers.
It was the last time he should ever see it,
And it was there. It would be waiting for him,
And it would understand why he came slowly,
For the last time. There was no science in that;
There was only a discreet benevolence
Of nature in his not having to make haste
Where death was leading him, and following him.
He could see death whenever he chose to look
Over his shoulder; for he felt him there,
And there was no need of seeing him too soon.
There were names all the way to Agatha's
For him to see; and death was, like himself,
Making no haste that day.

Part Second

                    Where it might come
Through many trees, there was late sunlight lying
On graves and grass; and everywhere a silence
Was like the coming of peace after pain.
He wondered if the dead were grateful for it,
And hoped they were. He was as far today
As ever he was from knowing more about it.
All that was best for him to know today
Was only that she was once a part of him,
And was a mystery that still humbled him
In his best memories. He was glad for them,
There in that silence, where he would not ask
How far he might be from deserving them.
He had not come to ask; he had come to tell her
What she must hear him say, and how his dream
Of long ago had latterly become
Another dream of now. The first had been
Of a long warfare in a field of death,
And of a noiseless victory; the second
Was one of those compelled necessities
Of righteousness for which the man appointed
Has God's mark on him and his work to do.
If Malory's God was not the King of Glory,
It was no less a king, whose voice foretold
Obedience where it fell; and it had fallen
Where manifestly it must be obeyed.
It was as plain as that to Malory,
And would be so to her, for whose repose

Obedience was exacted. Never in death,
More than in life, could there be such a sleep
As one that must not suffer some unrest
While one man was alive. If Nightingale
Were dead, and Malory dead, as Agatha was,
There would be peace. It was as plain as that
To Malory, moving there among the graves.

Now he could see time burning through the trees
With a slow crimson light that was, he reasoned,
The last of his last day that would be dying
Down to its end. Well, he was ready for that;
And it was better than a sunless day
Of clouds or rain would be. He could see now
A carved white name; and he began to see
More than a name, more than a shadowy face,
More than he came to find. For a flash of time
That was not measured she was there before him,
Between him and her house that had no door.
No shreds or clingings of a mortal change
Defiled or shadowed her serenity.
Her changing face and her mouse-colored hair,
Her solemn eyes that always laughed because
They saw so much that he was never to see—
Her mouth, and her white cheeks that were not white,
Her hands and feet, and all the rest of her,
Were there, and they were gone. But she was there,
And she was listening. So he told her all

Part Second

He knew—which was abysmally not all
There was to know. How far he must go back,
And by what unimaginable guidance,
To find himself in all his origins
Was more than science knew—which was as well,
Also, as other knowledge not for man.
He had not come to ask of Agatha
More than he knew.

                       "For one who has once had it,"
He told her, as an answer to her silence,
"Losing his faith in God is a disaster
By doubt still clouded and by nature made
Supportable. But to lose faith in man
And in himself, and all that's left to die for,
Is to feel a knife in his back before he knows
What's there, and then to know it was slimed first
With fiery poison to consume the friend
Who had no friend. It would have been as easy
To make me die instead of you, or with you,
But that would never have been enough for him.
He was not so enamoured of soft ways
As to do that. If someone else's neck
Was a good base whereon to set his feet
For a new spring to new vindictiveness,
There was no logic in his not using it.
Why else was a neck there? I warned him once,
That he might in some jungle of affairs

The Glory of the Nightingales

Tread inadvertently, and in the dark,
On a bad serpent, and it seems he did so;
Although his victim, then too much of a cripple
To sting him dead, has waited a long time.
Too long, as I can almost hear you saying,
Here in this dying light. I must leave all
To silence, and to justice after time—
Another justice that shall have its eyes,
As ours by time's necessity has not;
Which also may be well."

                    Her name had now
A dimness in a light that faded slowly
Into a twilight that would not last long;
And in the west he could see no more crimson
Through darker trees that suddenly were changed,
And stiller than they were. They were too still
To stay with, or to go from. With her name
For a companion, they were like all there was
Of home for him, who had no home on earth,
Or need of one. The time of his desire,
And of one other man's iniquity
Had yet one day's diminished length to fill
Before it was complete, and that was all.
Or was it all? Her name, assuring him,
Would answer nothing, and he would not ask.
He was not there to ask.

Part Second

                    "Now you have heard,"
He told her silently; "and having seen you,
I can see only one thing left to do.
I saw you for that moment, Agatha,
Which was enough, because it was no more."

He felt her glimmering name on the cold stone
With chilly fingers. There was only a name
There now; and he would leave it. On his way
From there, from Agatha, he was held a little
By two unhappy words that he could read
Where no trees blotted them: *Absalom Spinner.*
He scowled, and muttered; and for no new cause,
Felt to make sure of having in his pocket
His only wealth worth treasuring. He paused,
And in the dim light staring at that name,
Murmured, "It may not have been Nightingale,
So much as a too warm and willing bait.
There was a dereliction more primeval
Than his would be, and no affair of mine.
Spinner goes home to silence, as he went
Too many a time while she was fooling him,
And there may find some quiet. We don't know.
There is no quiet in life, and may be none
Till we may know that living is not dying.
There are two of us who may know more or nothing
Tomorrow. There is no room for us here.
There are two of us who are no longer wanted

The Glory of the Nightingales

Here at this cannibal banquet of man's life.
The word was given, and was not recalled;
And Agatha smiled."

                    He walked on, wondering
Why he was saying that, over and over:
"And Agatha smiled."

                    So on, and into Sharon,
He walked alone with night that had no eyes
To recognize him. He passed only strangers,
Nor many of them, though fifty thousand of them
Were not far off; and fifty thousand of them,
Or most of them, were only as many names,
Unknown to him. They might as well be names
On headstones, quiet as those he had left
Behind him in the dark, for all they were
To him; though he thought how each particular
Few feet and inches of unquiet life
That was a man or woman was for one
Or other, respectively, a more germane
And urgent work of God than was revealed
In others irremediably unlike it.
Annoyed that any such fond inanity
As that should be appointed to pursue him
And flick him like a moth along his last
Dark way through Sharon, he moved on unseen,
Or seen as nothing more felonious

Part Second

Than a man going somewhere by himself
On a calm starry evening, harmlessly.

Now in a street with trees on either side
That hid the stars, he paused, seeing not far
Ahead of him a house with lighted windows,
Telling of life within—but of what life,
Or whose, or of what scope or quality,
Revealing only what a curtain drawn
May show; for there were shadows passing on it,
As of some phantasmagorial invasion
Of a place that once was his, and Agatha's;
He had come from far away to look at it
Once more, and there it was, and was not his.
He would not make a feast of seeing it.
He did not even so much as know whose house
He looked at; and his memory was not asking
What drama of home was played by shadows now
Behind those curtains. He was not there to ask.
He was there to see a house for the last time;
And having seen it, he had seen all there was
For him to see in Sharon. When he left it,
There was one way more to go; and that way taken,
There was a mansion somewhere by the sea.

III

WITH his last piece of silver disappearing
To pay for his last food in a retreat
That harbored other derelicts in Sharon,
Malory saw the glimmering end of time
Going out, even while he saw new daylight coming
Indifferently through dawn-defying windows,
Unwashed and unashamed. It was a place
Accommodated more to his departure
Than to his entertainment or repose,
And one from which he went out willingly,
And gratefully, into the sunless light
Of a new morning that was not yet day,
And was not time. There was no longer need
Of time for him, more than there was of rest.
There was a way that he had come from Sharon,
And there was one from Sharon to the sea;
And there was nothing else on earth for him
Until he found the sea, and a new house
With towers and trees. That would be Nightingale's
New house; and Nightingale, he was informed,
Was in it, like a large and powerful worm
In a stone shell—a more pernicious mollusc,
With his hard house on land, than anything sunk
By God's foresight and love to live in the sea,
A stationary monster, doing no harm
And doing no good. Nightingale should have been
Like that—as God intended him to be,

And then forgot. So Malory must be fate,
Or more than fate, doing God's work, or fate's,
Or whatsoever the best name of it
Might be; for he was not pursuing words
This morning as he walked out finally
From Sharon towards the sunrise and the last
Of a long journey that would have an end
Where Nightingale was waiting in that house
Which he had always wanted, by the sea.

Like a fire to burn the world, with all its anguish,
And with all its evil evidence of man,
Malory saw the sun and saw it rising
For the last time, he said; and that was well.
In a world that would not burn there was no reason
Why a flash, and an immediate way out,
Should be delayed for two that were too many
To be alive and would be valued more
For being dead. He felt the gratefulness
Of nature for so right a thought as that,
And the approval of the rising sun;
He felt the spur of a good going forward
To the right end—a prize of realization
Withheld from all but the more fortunate
Whose dreams are preparations. Malory walked
In common shoes as Hermes might have walked
In wingèd sandals when he was not flying;
And every step that was away from Sharon

The Glory of the Nightingales

Was nearer to the sea.

                    He tramped along,
Securely, with an onward earnestness,
And with a purpose in his expedition,
That might not from the curious be concealed.
He was not one of the world-nourishing
Unnoticeables who fit the place that finds them
And are not feverish to find another;
Nor was he one with any claim or station
Among the vagabonds, who would have marked him
As a man scratched, a gentleman gone down,
And going still. He would be one of those
Who in their unrevealed appearances
Are more distinguished than they are distinct,
And therefore are not welcome in the fold
Of the old brotherhood. It was not so
When Malory was himself, and now it mattered
Little, if anything, what a brother man
Might think of him. If there should be no thought,
So much the better. Malory would attend
To as much thinking of his own enigma
As was imperative or expedient;
And a man saying that was not at odds
With his obscurity.

                    An hour or so
Away from Sharon, none of the few faces

That were abroad so early would be one
To recognize, or to be reckoned with
In terms of amiable embarrassment
Begotten of mischance; and it was good
When he could say that such an hour or so
Was dead, and well behind him. It was early,
And he was free—with all the wealth there was.
For him, in one small weapon that was his.
Croesus had nothing now but a rich name
That left him poor. Malory was like God.
So far as there was life to be considered,
He was omnipotent; and as for dying,
Death was another country where new light
Or darkness would inevitably prevail.
If there was hazard in his tearing down
This treacherous and imperfect house of man,
There was a moment of magnificence,
No less, in which the worst part of the world
Would make a piece of history best forgotten,
Along with his, that soon would follow it
Where history goes. It was as plain as that
To Malory, and so early in the morning
That hours to come were only coming names
Of time, the grave of names. This afternoon,
So far ahead of him, was only a name,
Because it was not yet; and what it held
For Malory was a picture that he saw
Because it should be there. The best and worst

Of pictures that we draw before we see them
Are there like that.

                      With none to challenge him,
And only few to stare a moment at him
As at a stranger too much on his way
To pay for salutation, he walked on
With more than half of Sharon still asleep
Behind him. There was only one more distance
Between him and the end. The rest were done,
And were among the journeys men have taken
So long ago that we shall see no roads
To say where those men went. As hours became
Forgotten but implacable recruits
Of his pursuing past, the name of Sharon
Was that of a dead city far behind him;
And as he walked the end was always with him,
And he was always nearer to the sea—
Till now it was full noon. He would soon have
The shadow of himself for company,
Not asking or imagining for how long
Some other shadows had attended him,
Or what they were. All he had seen of late,
All he saw now, was real—of a true form
And of a substance undeniable;
Or all but Agatha, and she was real.
There were no shadows or illusions waiting
In Nightingale's unnecessary mansion

To make him pause; for there was Nightingale,
Who was no shadow, and was deplorably
No phantom or illusion. He was as real
As reptiles, or as wolves are in dark places
Where men go perilously and unsuspecting
Of what else may be there till they are torn
By claws they cannot see. There were no doubts
Or reservations to be spent and wasted
On what he sought and was to find before
The sun went down. It was not going yet,
And Malory knew the sea was not far off.
There would be more light left than he should need;
And when it was all done, there would be light
For those who came to see.

              A giant elm,
Whose height from somewhere out of memory
Came back as yesterday an oak had come,
Told him how far away the desert wreck
Of a storm-buried past was from him now;
And a blank vision of oblivion
Chilled him with an irrelevance of regret
That he should never see that elm again—
As if a landmark had a language older
Than his, and a long eloquence that only
Ruin could understand. He saw behind him
Its height and silence; and as he moved on,
He could see all there ever was of Sharon

The Glory of the Nightingales

Fading into a distance that was death;
For there was no more time now than an hour
Between him and the sea; and afternoon,
Which earlier was a name for time unborn,
Was here, and it would soon be growing old.
Malory saw before him, drawn already
By fate, a place he need not hurry to see,
So long as it was there and was the place
Where he was going. Nightingale was there,
And any place where there was Nightingale,
Today, was a good place for Malory.

There was no need of asking whose it was
When Malory found it. Like a magician's work,
Or the small castle of a little king,
He saw it among trees, and saw the towers
Of which he had been told. He was not held
By them, or long impressed. He had not come
To study them; he had come to see the man
Who was inside, or in the neighborhood—
If such as he had neighbors. The whole place
Told of an empty wealth of loneliness
More than of hospitality and friends.
There might be satellites who deceived themselves
As friends, but they would never deceive the man
Within, who may have opened his heavy doors,
For conscience' sake, to anyone who might flatter
His host with an adroitness to be borne,

And help him to forget. He would soon forget,
Said Malory; and he waited for a door
To open, thinking of two other doors
That soon would open to an older house,
Where all men go.

               Waiting inside, he saw
More wealth, attesting an intelligence
That was another lonely waste. He felt it
In all there was about him; and for surety
Of his possession and determination,
He touched, with fingers that were not afraid
To find it there, a more sufficient wealth
In his own pocket. He was a richer man
Than Nightingale. He was the richest man
In this poor world. He was a king, whose word
Was life or death, until another door
Was opened and the voice of a lost friend—
The voice of a dead friend, he must remember—
Called him as if a boy that he had known
And loved at school were calling him in pain,
For which there was no cure. Across more years
Than men had lived he heard it calling him,
With all but the authority of youth
To make it young. There was a humor in it
That had the sound of knowledge mocking hope,
And wonder sharing certainty with doubt;
And there was more in it than had a name

For vengeance to invent. And when it said,
"Malory, are you there!" it had the sound
It might have had if in the mills of years
Another life than Malory's had been broken.

IV

LIKE a desolating cry of an old music,
Long unheard, and falling strange in a new place,
Came again the searching voice of one appointed
To be voiceless; and an ache in Malory's heart
Was a poison that would soon be half a sorrow
If he waited; and he waited. He must act,
Or a folly more to be disowned and loathed
Than fear would slowly strangle resolution
With hands invisible and with silky fingers
Stronger than fate. And where was fate, meanwhile,
To leave him unresolved and hesitating
Till he was hearing "Malory, are you there,"
For a third time, and hearing it unanswered,
As if there were no answer? He was there,
At last, and opportunity was with him,
And he had yet no answer but his presence,
Which a few steps towards an open door
Revealed. With his hand clutching hidden death,
He stood and saw the man whom he had come
So far to kill, and waited, saying nothing,
As he gazed there at one who had grown older
Than time had made him.

                        In a velvet robe,
And in a prisoner's chair that was on wheels,
Nightingale was half sitting and half lying,
So nearly a pale prey of death already

That Malory's hand, still hidden in his coat,
Held nothing but his hate. The face he saw
Staring at his and waiting for some word,
Was that of one whom he had honored once
With love and trust, and with a grateful envy
That would have yielded all but life itself
To pay for such a friend. The same dark eyes
Were burning at him with a lower fire
From a white face that he had never seen
Before. The face that he had loved and hated
Was not the face he saw. The bones were there
That formerly were buried under power
And grace, and there was as much more of it
As time and pain together had not shrunk
To skin and death. In youth's idolatry
There was no possibility of this;
And in the fires of wreck and revelation,
Nothing had been foreseen that was like this—
Which was unfair. It was not even fair fate,
Said Malory; and he waited for an answer
To his appearance. He had not come to ask,
He had come to act; and as he was not acting,
He waited. There was nothing for him to say
That moved his tongue, and he had best be going,
If the rich gold of expectation yielded
Only a dross like this. He looked away
From the wan wreck before him to three walls
Tiered high with books that held the best of man's

Part Fourth

Creation and reflection for the solace
Of this thing in a chair that went on wheels,
And to a fourth wall that was most a window,
Framing a sea and sky for Nightingale
To watch and contemplate, and to see pictured
With shipwreck and remorse. He had always wanted
A place like this; and having a large habit
Of seeing as his what most it was he wanted,
Now he could have the sky and the wide ocean
Together, and in a chair that went on wheels,
He could sit still and see them all day long.
There was no need of killing him; he was dead
Before his name was called.

                          "Well, Malory,"
Said Nightingale, with questions in his eyes
And in his voice, "the old mariner's ashore;
Look at him, and you'll see him at the end
Of his last cruise. You may as well have a chair
And see him comfortably. If you have come
To shoot him, he will not be disagreeable,
Or argumentative. If I surprise you
With a mistaken levity, and a notion
That's all outside your proper meditation,
Forgive me. But experience, I have found,
Encourages an imaginative caution;
Though caution, I may guess, would serve me now
As a thin armor. I might ring a bell,

But who should answer it in time to save you
From a superfluous incarceration,
And me from a good sleep? I don't sleep well,
Malory; and if truth has painted you
As you look now, you are not of the seven.
I wonder what you have there in your pocket,
More than a hand. Again I'll ask your pardon
If my imagination is in error;
And then, if you may care, I'll tell you why
It was that you brought visions in with you,
And some that were not lovely."

                                        Malory sighed,
As one discomfited by destiny
Too shrewd for chance, and said to Nightingale,
"I see no reason left why you should live,
Or why I should stay longer. You had always
Too much of an unused intelligence
To be as you are now; and you have still
Enough to need the word of no physician
To say where you are going. If there's hell,
Of one sort or another, and there may be,
You will not be much older than you are
Before you know. Or, it is possible
That yours was here."

                        "I see," said Nightingale.
"A doctor, to be more than wind and hope,

Must have three eyes. Well, you may have your fee
For asking—or without."

                              Malory moved
Along indifferently, and at the window
Stood looking at the ocean, which he saw
As men had seen it who were not yet men.
In ages lost in the long void of time,
It must have tossed and foamed as helplessly
As now, at the wind's will; and to the eyes
Of Malory's unimagined ancestors
It must have been a fearsome mystery,
Filled with infernal things in ancient fancy,
As it was now in fact. Look as he would,
Life was a fabrication of the demons,
On land, or in the sea, or in the air.
A snake, seeing a man, could frighten him
And sting him to quick death; and a small fly
Could sting him to slow death, and with no aid
Of dream or fancy. A far smaller thing
Than a small fly had shattered Nightingale;
And he was dying in his grand new house,
Which he had always wanted, near the ocean.
A tired bacteriologist, seeing him there,
Might say there was a God. Nature, at least,
Had never done her work so well before,
Or saved a man of science so much trouble.
A sense of rest, and of an unforeseen

Release replenished him with a new wish
To live—a wish that had in it more wonder
Than satisfaction. A new fear of living
Had come to him who had no fear of dying,
Or wish to die, or means to live. He wondered
How such a warfare of inept negations
Might end—when for a moment, having turned
Himself to look at Nightingale again,
He fancied he was in the way of knowing
Immediately of that; for the first sight
That held him was no invalid in a chair,
But a black weapon pointing silently
Straight at him. He considered the short barrel,
And then the square pale face of Nightingale,
Grinning mysteriously and ominously,
More like a living mask on a dead face
Than like a face alive. But Nightingale
Was living, and for the nonce, apparently,
Was finding life a privilege and a pleasure.

"Forgive me, Malory, if I'm curious,"
He said, "but I've a leprosy to know
What you have in that pocket where your hand is.
This thing of mine—it was not always mine—
Is educated and almost alive,
And might have speech. Now let me look at yours,
And I will tell you then which implement
I like the better of the deadly two.

I may want both of them, if yours is pretty—
Like Absalom's. Are you surprised, somewhat?
Let me have yours, and I'll say how it was,
And why, and all about it. You are not going
To kill me in this chair and have a mess.
I can see that."

      "I came down here for that,"
Malory answered, "and I came too late.
Nature has beaten me. Nature, or God;
I don't know which. I have no need of this."

"I thank you, Malory." Nightingale, still grinning,
Had a flat pistol now in each thin hand,
And held them aimed at Malory. "Now sit down.
With your permission I'll say these are mine,
Although I do not use them. They are pretty,
And I have always loved the beautiful;
And the most beautiful of all there was
On earth you stole from me. But we'll go back
To that. Now this one in my other hand
Was given to me, and gladly, by a friend
Who came one day, as you have come this day,
To make an end of me. Yes—Absalom.
He had magnified himself with wicked gin,
And I was not like this. I was on my feet.
I smiled at him, and I said, 'Absalom,
You cannot kill me without having a drink

With me in my new house.' He hesitated,
And I held out my hand. He wanted rum
More than he wanted me, and did not know it
Until he was informed—though I 'll not boast
Of any too brisk a sureness at the time,
Or say that I was happy to be waiting
So much at his not all assuring service.
I was not comfortable while I waited,
But I was calm. 'Absalom,' I suggested,
'There 's a whole world of things for me to tell you,
But first we 'll have a drink in my new house—
A tall, strong, curative drink made long ago,
An endless and illuminating drink,
Before I make of you a shining man,
A free man, and a merrier citizen
Than you have seen yet in your looking-glass.'"

"Yes," Malory said, "you could afford, perhaps,
As much as that, or more. I have not been
So far from news of life that not a word
Of you has found me. I have known more of you
Than a man has to know to be advised
Of honor wasted, as mine was on yours,
That I called honor. I leave men's affairs
That are not mine to men whose part it is
To manage them with a safe decency.
But when a friend . . . Why am I saying this?
Why am I here, with all I came to do

Part Fourth

So nearly done before me. Absalom's wife—
Where is she now? I know where Absalom is,
For I have seen his grave."

                    "If you saw that,"
Said Nightingale, amiably, "you saw the stone
That I placed over him. Ophelia's father
Had a good end, or she believed he had,
And so had Absalom. As for his wife,
A moment of indulgence and attention
Will heal your implications in one error
That cries for healing. She was not a wife;
She was a fruity sort of Cyprian fungus,
With arms and legs, the brain-pan of a chicken,
And all the morals of a pleasant monkey.
God in his wisdom, which is infinite,
And is not ours, has always made such things
To be consumed. They are for nothing else,
And are good for nothing else; and if they could,
They would be nothing else. Send them to school,
And see what they learn there. Give them a home,
And see what's left of it when they have had it
Long enough to be tired of living in it.
They are not happy, or not so for long,
And that's a pity—or may be a warning
For all the others, who are interested
But not at large. When you ask where she is,
You may as well be asking for the story

Of all the rest of them. She's not in Sharon;
And Sharon has not seen her since a time
When Absalom, failing to assassinate her,
And losing half his face, did me the honor
Aforesaid. So for God's sake, Malory,
Whatever you do to me, or to my name,
Let Absalom Spinner's name be one to shine
As that of one man who had what he wanted.
Absalom came to make a feast of me,
And went away, or rather was carried away,
To sleep without a memory or a care,
Until he woke to find a longer feast
Awaiting him than I should ever have made.
I fixed a competent annuity
On Absalom, who made one splendid leap
From Sharon into paradise, and remained.
He was illuminated for three years
With light that never revealed him to himself
As a poor wick that he must saturate
Unceasingly in order not to see it.
He was a panorama and a pageant
That would have been an eminence in a city
Greater than Sharon. He was joy and color
Where nothing has been like him since he went.
As long as he could play, Spinner was trumps—
And always won. His only currency
Worth counting in his triumph was a freedom
To be a fool; and he had more of it

Than he could lose. Spinner had everything,
And had it for three years in tropic bloom.
Before it might have faded, or become
Only an occupation, or a duty,
Absalom died. He fell down under a dray,
And died. With his beginnings and ideals,
And the Lord watching him, giving him first
Some brief and beneficial misery
For joy to come, his cup was alabaster,
And it was always full until it cracked,
And the glad juice ran out. No, Malory,
Never defeat your sympathies or regrets
With Absalom. Lay roses on his grave,
But do not desecrate them with your tears;
For Absalom, wherever he is, may see you.
You may go round the world, and round again,
And after that you may go round once more
For sight of as inexhaustible a cask
Of happiness as Absalom, and not find it."

Malory sighed, and was almost asleep
With weariness. He had not known how tired
A weight that has at last been lifted leaves him
Who carries it too far. But he could say
To Nightingale, half hearing his own words,
"You are the last of men, as I know men,
To make so easy a simplicity
Of lives that are not yours. If your condition

The Glory of the Nightingales

Is a best evidence of your playful ethics,
You are less fortunate than Absalom—
Who, in his way, was as unusual
As you are, Nightingale. I have seen life,
And have not seen it easy. I have seen death.
Yes, Nightingale; I have seen death, also."

"Yes, Malory," said Nightingale, distinctly,
And with a resignation of assent,
"You have seen death. You are looking at it now,
And to your inexpressible satisfaction.
I know it; and I 've had cataracts of ideas
Descending on me, and to some effect,
Since you came in. There 's been a trickle of them
Before; and we 'll say more of them tomorrow."

"I don't know. I am going," Malory said,
And rose, only to find that his knees bent
Like hinges in the legs of a lay-figure.
He sat, or fell, into his chair again,
And there forgot to say where he was going.
He did not know. He was too tired to care.

V

IN the morning, in the light of a sun shining
On a million little waves that flashed and danced
With a cold primordial mockery there below him
And beyond him, beyond sight or thought of him,
Or of Nightingale, whose hospitality
Was like a venomous food that a blind man
Had eaten in his weariness, Malory looked
Away into the distance and found only
Distance. He was an outcast long at home
With distances, but never with one like this
That was before him now. He was alive,
And was to have been dead with Nightingale,
Who sat with death already; he was awake,
And he could see too clearly and too far,
Or so he thought, over an empty ocean
Into an empty day, and into days
That were to come and must be filled somehow
With other stuff than time. There would be friends
In Sharon to acknowledge him so far
As on his word to see him on his way
To somewhere else. There was no fiery need
Of being a fool, and he must let the past
Serve as it would the present and the future;
Which was a way of saying that he must have
A few reviving dollars. He had eaten
Nightingale's food only to give him strength
To go without it, and would have no more.

The Glory of the Nightingales

"There's one thing in this Christian life of ours,
  Which none of us could live, engages me,"
  Nightingale said to Malory, coming down
  To say some formal words and then to go.
"I mean the other cheek—in moderation.
  You are a doctor, and that's why you know
  What happens to a man who walks all day,
  And doesn't eat till he's too tired to care
  If anyone eats. I sent it up to you
  Before you should see me. You called it tact,
  Perhaps, but fear was nearer the right name.
  I was afraid that you might emigrate
  In anger when you found yourself awake
  In one of my not execrable beds.
  No matter what I've been, what's left of me
  Is human; and if you have Christian faith,
  Or Christian curiosity, sufficient
  Unto some other evil day than this,
  You may lay treasures up—if not in heaven,
  Then here on earth, which is another matter—
  Treasures not for yourself. I'm no such ass
  As innocence like that would make of me,
  Though I've been worse. I want you in this house
  Until tomorrow. You are in no haste now—
  Now you have seen that I am not worth killing,
  And you will do yourself and me a service
  If you will not run off immediately.

For, Malory,"—his mouth trembled—"there's not going
To be much time."

        "There will be time enough,"
Malory said, "to make you call to Christ
For less. I can do nothing about that.
I can say nothing that will give you hope,
Or happiness. I am sorry that you must live,
And think, until you die; and you have there
The sum of all the grief there is in me
For rather less than a fair reckoning.
Why, in God's name, should you be asking me
To stay, and watch? Am I so medieval
As to enjoy seeing even my worst friend
Suffer too long? I'd be no better for that."

Nightingale tapped the wheels that held his chair,
And looked across the waves. Then, with a smile
Of understanding that had no reproach,
He turned again to look at Malory:
"You have a right to say it with an edge,
And I have none to mind your saying it.
Some follow lights that they have never seen,
And I was given a light that I could see
But could not follow. There's the devil in that,
Always; and that's why I am asking you
To stay until tomorrow. If the food
That you have eaten here distresses you,

Pay for it, and forget it. It was yours.
I have a sum of money that is yours,
And I can see no honor-gnawing harm
In your belated repossession of it;
For you were robbed of it as viciously
As if you had been gagged and strangled for it.
But that's a tune that I was to play later,
If you would stay and listen. I saw your eyes
When you came yesterday to finish me,
And knew that you would stay. I don't know why
A man's condition makes a difference,
But so it is. Somehow it is not done,
Or not by Malory. For a glance at me
Told him how more proficient an assassin
Fate was than any doctor. You will stay,
If only for a suffering abstraction
Misnamed humanity. I don't mean myself,
And you are in no haste."

                    "I'm in no haste,"
Said Malory, "and I don't know what you mean—
Or all you mean. I know that I was robbed,
And share my knowledge willingly with you.
That was a part of it, but far from all.
You spoke of it, and may do as much more
As your interpretation of affairs
Compels or counsels. I had not come for that,
Or painted my bare walls with expectations."

"I see," said Nightingale. "You saw so far
Beyond a small recovery of the past
That all was in the present. Naturally
You had not come for that. I never fancied
That you were here for that. For when you came,
I saw you as you looked when we were boys
Together at school; and in a flash I saw
What you had learned of me in other schools.
I'm sorry, Malory, that the world goes round
The sun in such a way as to leave time
So far behind it; or I should be sorry,
If I saw less. I see more, possibly,
Than you see, Malory. If you had shot me,
You would have seen a finite retribution
That would have done no good. It's not like that.
You might as well have shot the flying earth
To kill a system—of which you are part,
And so the whole. But that's not Agatha."

His calm eyes for a moment were like those
Of an expectant and confessed offender.
But there was nothing done, and nothing said,
Till Malory spoke: "I will hear anything
That you may say to me of Agatha,
And your destruction of her. You destroyed her
With hell's deliberation in your method,
Or I'm as wrong as hell. You cannot say

That I am wrong. You may have been the devil,
But you were never a fool."

                "I beg of you,
Malory, to believe me when I swear
That I was more than one. I was a college
Of fools, under one scalp and in one skin.
But I was not myself. That's an old plaster,
And one that has been used till it will stick
No longer. You are right, for you were saying
Just about that." Nightingale closed his eyes,
As if a picture of his thoughts had hurt him.
Malory watched the sea.

               For a long time
There was a stillness as of all things said,
And of a waiting for no other end
Than evident farewell. But Nightingale
Said quietly, at last, "No, Malory,
There were no diagrams of your disaster
Drawn to include what came, or half of it.
Yet, when it came . . ."

              "Yes, Nightingale—when it came.
You were not there in Sharon when it came.
You were not there again till we were gone—
All three of us. They are not made of iron,
Women like her; though many of them are stronger

In stronger ways than ours. She and her child
Should not have gone so early, Nightingale.
If it was best for them to go together,
It was not then. They would be here today
If you had been—yourself. I can say that,
As well as you, for I was not myself,
And am not yet. There was a devil waiting
To steal me from myself. You are no part
Of that, although you may have been a devil.
I think you must have been one, Nightingale,
For you were not a man in a man's way.
It was some time before we found that out,
And you had not come back. If you had come . . .
I am glad not to know. If you had come,
We might not be here as we are today—
Which might be better. It could not well be worse
For you, or more ridiculous for me.
It is almost a pity that you're not able
To savor properly the humor of this."

"God's right is yours," Nightingale answered, slowly,
And with no frown of protest, "to be bitter.
Yet, Malory, we'll see what there is left.
There may be more than you are willing to see,
If seen too near. I doubt if any of this
Is new, for I dare say it has all happened
In Samarcand or Celebes before us.
Should even a smouldering of apology

The Glory of the Nightingales

Be living in that, extinguish it at once
With indignation, hatred, or contempt.
You cannot hate me any harder now
Than heretofore, though you might find an anger
Somewhere in you that has not yet been used.
But I'll hope not; and I shall say but little
Of Agatha, and that only by your leave.
I said that when I saw you standing there,
When you came yesterday, I saw you first
As I had seen you long ago at school,
When we were boys together, never dreaming
Of what the coming men in us had waiting.
There was nothing then of mine that was not yours;
And you, if I had asked it, would have given
More than you had to give. You would have found
Outside your own possession what you lacked,
If possible, and you would have called it mine.
I should have done no less, and should have said
That a friend who so failed me was a liar—
A thing without a day's worth of remembrance
Left in him for my eyes. In those unfledged
Omniscient years of youth, I knew myself
Better, sometimes, than was a joy for me;
For there were premonitions then, and warnings.
I saw myself a part of a small world
Of traps and lies and fights and compromises,
And saw beyond it while I saw it coming,
And welcomed it—although I measured it

For what it was; and hating it, even then,
Precociously, I have not always loved
Myself. I had enough of other vision
To see the other side of selfishness,
But I had not the will to sacrifice
My vanity for my wits. I was the law—
And here I am. Here I am not the law.
I saw you, Malory, in those same raw years,
As far from me, in dreams and differences,
As ever you got; and that was a long way.
You were a thin-skinned prodigy of science
Before you had a whisker. You were never
A doctor; you had not the hide for it,
And you had no authoritative aura
To make a poor sick citizen glad for you
And God in the same room. You learned as much
Before you were too old; and I believe
My foresight and affection aided you
In your inquisitive enmity to microbes."

"You led me to a door that had no key
For me to use until you gave me one,"
Malory said; "and you made possible
A place where I might never have arrived
Without your foresight and your confidence.
Good God—your confidence!" Malory poured
A powerful drink of whiskey for himself,
And drank it with a purpose.

The Glory of the Nightingales

                    "You have lifted
Rather too much of that abused nepenthe,
Since you became a question-mark in Sharon,"
Said Nightingale, with his eye on the bottle;
"But it will do your body and soul no manner
Of harm today. You may not care tomorrow
Whether or no the ocean's made of it.
We'll see—or you will. So you found at last
Your niche of honor in the living temple,
Which is a place worth finding. I found one,
Also, in which I stood more gloriously
Mistaken for a beneficial hero
Than anyone else in town. I did some good,
And brought a sound and honorable name
Out of the dust and cobwebs of decay.
My father, a most melodious Nightingale,
Sang more songs than were good for a good bird,
And I was the indemnifying phoenix.
I was a youth of parts and promises,
Endowed with a convenient fluid conscience
That covered the best of me with a bright varnish,
And made me shine. If none had thwarted me,
I might be shining still, instead of dying
In this expensive nest. If I had learned,
In time, to know that I was not the law
That made me live, I should have done more shining,
And in a light more grateful to my eyes.
I was a sort of Saint George in the town,

However, as years went on; and I slew dragons
Habitually, having a spear of gold
Which I had fashioned of my own endeavor
And sharpened with commendable incentive.
That was all right, and it was all as easy
As it was right. I made a better town
Of Sharon, and I never sang outside
Myself the song in me that I knew best.
Why should I sing it? No one asked for it,
And only the envious and inefficient
Would have enjoyed it. I was not so bad,
So long as I was having my own way.
It 's a grave matter for the commonwealth,
Sometimes, when a good egoist goes down,
Whether he goes invisibly, as I did,
Or with the flags and tatters of defeat
Thrown after him. But that was all to be,
And I was waiting, eminent and unwarned,
Serene in Sharon. I was the dominant bird,
Outsinging and outshining and outflying
Everything else. I was informed one day
That in my doing what no one else would do,
I was a cold magician and a seer;
And that, for whistling, gold would follow me.
It did—though not till I had followed first,
While others whistled. It was easy then
For me to be magnificent and agreeable,
For I had still to learn how heavy a cake

The Glory of the Nightingales

A king may have to eat. Before I learned,
I was a lord of a small firmament,
Or almost that, with fifty thousand stars,
Most of them having a face that beamed on me,
We'll say, with more approval than reproof;
And that was right. I had robbed no man then,
And no man had robbed me. I was untried
In my submissions and humilities.
I was unquestioned of my qualities.
I was a friend to many who would have had
No eyes to see me had their place been mine.
I was a more approachable Maecenas
Than always had the license of his judgment.
I knew that I had played with the same cards
That were for all to use, and played them better.
I was a prodigal father's thrifty son,
With wisdom to be generous in my thrift.
I was a man the more to be admired
For tempering admiration with respect,
Or with a gracious imitation of it.
I was a man aware that each man carried
Only the lamp the Lord had given to him.
I raised myself no higher than others held me,
And therefore was a brother who understood.
I was a light that would be shining always,
A light for generations to remember.
I was a sort of permanent morning star.
I was the Glory of the Nightingales.

Part Fifth

The sinful, well-intentioned Nemesis
Who said that first—it must have been a woman—
Should have had spiders in her marmalade,
And scorpions every morning in her stockings.
I was the Glory of the Nightingales!
Give me a drink, and don't say it will kill me.
You know damned well it won't. Only too well
You know it won't—and don't say you're a doctor.
I told you about time, and the earth moving.
Arthritis and Ataxia—two Alphas,
And a malevolent long alphabet
Between them and Omega."

                    Malory stared
At Nightingale, partly in admiration,
Partly in helpless wonder and regret
For such a fusion of mortalities
To make one death. Where was the use of power,
If a wrong element in the beginning
Was to make this of it? Where was the use
Of satisfaction, hatred, or revenge,
If life avenged itself? If it did, always,
There would be justice hidden somewhere in it;
But if the weak and headstrong and untried
Paid for the rest to let the play go on—
If there was more fragility and defeat
Hiding in one disordered competence
Than in a thousand safe complacencies,

The Glory of the Nightingales

Having not much to hide or to reveal—
Why was it better not to be a dog?
A tired bacteriologist might ask
As much of Nightingale—or of himself.
He had not asked. He had not come to ask.
He had been tried, and had as little to say
Of one discrepancy as of another.
He was no longer critical. He saw
Too near the end—forgetting how many ends
There are that are not death.

                      "No, Malory,"
Said Nightingale, returning from a silence,
"I'm not composing an apology.
I was looking at the sea. Apology
Would be a worse offence to you than any
That you have suffered yet of my invention;
And I have been inventive, even as Cain
Was active. I've been drenched until I smelt
With praise of it. Fathers have made a show
Of my initiative for their dull sons
To copy, and have clucked at my foresight
In seizing what another could not see.
It is not always criminal to be first,
But there's a poison and a danger waiting
For him who will not hear, and will not listen,
While choruses of inner voices tell him
When to be second. That was the curse prepared

Part Fifth

For me: I would not listen to my voices.
I'll only say it was not wholly strange
That I did not. When Agatha came to Sharon,
I saw what all my prowlings had been worth,
And what my restlessness had waited for.
It was not hard for me to find my way
To her acquaintance. I was not unknown,
Or notably unaccepted or unsought;
I was so far from that as to be shown
To strangers as one having everything —
Which was not so. The one thing I had not
Was everything, and she was Agatha.
But all was going well, and I believed
My triumph, long so empty of what most
It had so perilously lacked, would soon
Be filled, and all my turmoil and unrest
Be quieted. I should have everything —
In truth as in report; and that was all
I asked. The wonder of it, Malory,
Is that I should have had it, or I think so,
If in my self-destroying adoration
Of my divinity, I had not brought you
To see me at my worship, and see also
The object of it. Kismet, or Ananke,
Or melancholy chance, was following me
When I brought you, as a friend brings a friend
Into his treasure-house, to Agatha.
You were my king of friends, and Agatha

[57]

The Glory of the Nightingales

Was to be queen of all there was of me
And mine to give her. There was no fool's dream
In my delusion, for I was not a fool—
Not then; and Agatha was not a dream—
Not then. I was as near to paradise
As man may be. It was you who shut the door.
It was you who stood between me and the door.
Yes, it was you who made a knave of me,
When I was almost . . ."

                "You were almost—what?"
Malory asked. "Are you the only knave
Who has—almost—made a good woman love him?
I fancy there are one or two before you
In the lost archives of iniquity,
For you are not unique in having a way.
You might, with all your batteries of allegiance,
Devotion, adoration, and insistence,
Have stilled within her for a while her voices—
Which were as many as yours—and I don't know
That in some web of pity and hesitation
She might not have been caught, to find herself
Your—queen, it was, you called her. Nightingale,
She would have been the most afflicted queen
That ever reigned, if she had reigned with you.
She never said to me as much as that;
A few infrequent and unwilling words
To which you might have listened, and agreed,

Part Fifth

Told all her story. She was sorry for you,
Nightingale, but she saw too many of you.
All which would not have mattered, I suppose
If love had shared her caution, and told lies
Enough to her about it, but your Kismet,
Or your Ananke, had no power or skill
To do love's work for you. Love was not there.
You knew it was not there, but you would hear
No voice, or none at first, but vanity's.
Later, you may have heard God knows what voices;
For all your nonsense of my shutting doors
To your phantasmal paradise is worthy
Of a mad weakling. I'll be generous now,
When nothing comes of it, and call you mad—
Though you are not. If I have called you weak,
Say when it was, and ask your memory
If you are still inventive. I know traits
Of more malignities in mortal growth
Than you have heard of, and I know their names;
But not one of an ulcered understanding
That you possessed once, or that possessed you,
Of even the first of human rudiments.
You are the one physician, Nightingale,
For seizures, and peculiar paroxysms
That are not yet established or observed
In books or clinics. If you have healed yourself
Too late, you have done something for your soul
That even your stricken body will acknowledge,

The Glory of the Nightingales

If only with more pain. Why should I stay
To watch fate doing my work? I can do nothing."

"You might, by watching fate, do a deal more
  Than you came here to do," said Nightingale,
  With a long frown that held a weary smile:
"Unless you have a mind to drown yourself
  In my commodious ocean, Malory,
  You will do well to stay. You must, indeed,
  For long enough to let me go on saying
  What I began. You interrupted me,
  And you were well within your injured rights.
  You see how pliable and how mild I am,
  And wonder, maybe, if it's all my conscience.
  I should not say it was. I should say, rather,
  It was acknowledgment and recognition,
  Humility and surrender. It's more than that,
  And has to do with more than you and me—
  But that will come. You bit my words away
  When I said I was almost . . . Well, I was.
  I was, till you took everything there was
  Alive for me to live for. You had science,
  And I had nothing without Agatha.
  It was the gash of that awakening
  That would not heal. Surprise and unbelief
  Tortured it, and slow hate infected it.
  A venom in me that I had not before
  Believed in—one that I had said and sworn

Was not there—made its way infernally
Into the last and darkest crevices
That were concealed in me to be explored
And torn. I had not known there were such places
Anywhere, till a devil discovered them
With his contaminated little needle
Of hate. He may have visited you later,
Malory, and you may have come from Sharon
Down here because he sent you. If he sent you,
He was forestalled by power stronger than his,
And vengeance more sublime. Strong as he is,
The devil is only a part of destiny,
Doing the worst he may. He deceives man,
And makes an idiot shambles of the world
About so often, and for the joy of seeing
What fools men are; and whether he sees us here
At war or peace, he flies and strikes and stings
Incessantly, and has a name for peace
That pleases him. Men would have said, and women,
That I was, of all men, or should have been,
The most at peace and the least agitated
By the surprises of necessity.
That was my way of showing myself to men,
And women; and that was how I looked to you,
And Agatha. You had taken everything
Away from me, but that was how I looked.
All that I almost had was gone before
I knew who had it; and when at last I knew,

The Glory of the Nightingales

I was alone with my incredulousness.
I saw myself as one left robbed and stabbed
By friends who had betrayed him in the dark.
I wandered in the dark for many days
And many nights before I found my way;
And there was not a soul in Sharon knew
What I was finding; and I did not know,
At first, what I had found. I was to know,
Thoroughly, only when as a physician,
As you so unprofessionally suggested,
I made a proper search and diagnosis
Of what the devil within me had been doing.
When devils have driven their stings in deep enough,
And done their work, knowledge has time to mourn."

"But why the devil do you insist so hard
  On devilish help in your duplicity?"
  Malory asked, and scowled at Nightingale.
"You knew your work, and what was coming of it,
  Or might come. I am leaving myself out,
  This time, and I'm not saying what came to me—
  Though I had devils enough assisting me
  To my destruction—if you must have devils."

"If I'm impervious to insinuation,"
  Nightingale said, "you called me a physician.
  And if I shall appear to you, perchance,
  More a physician than a penitent,

Part Fifth

You will know why. If it would help the past,
I'd get down somehow on my knees to you,
And you would not like that; for it would make you
Merely a little sick, and be a trial
For me. I doubt if either of us would like
Ourselves as well for such extravagance.
I can afford, I fear, no more declension
Of my interior esteem, or dwindling
Of what there's left in me of dignity.
I had some once, and many may have said
I wore it with a comfort as becoming
As it was native. I don't know just what
They're saying now in Sharon. I'm not there.
About the time you left was the right time
For me to be away. When I returned
To find you gone, and Agatha gone before you,
I learned at last, as for the first time, wholly,
And comprehensively, what I had done.
There were no plans or diagrams, remember,
In my invention. How should I be certain,
I asked, of what might happen if I should knock
Some props away that held some walls upright?
There was no way of knowing. The house might stand
For ever, or might slant and sway a little,
And still survive, and stand. How should I know,
For sure, what houses were ordained to stay
Upright, no matter what storms broke over them,
Or what was taken away from under them?

[63]

The Glory of the Nightingales

Your legacy, which you needed, was for you
A large one. It was a gift out of God's hand,
Agatha said, and may have believed it was.
I don't know that it was n't. My advice
Told you to sink it all, and more than all,
Where I was confident, and, as I saw it,
Magnanimous. I sank as much as yours
In the same hole, believing wealth would rise
And flow like golden lava out of it—
By far the worst inspired of my not many
Mistakes in seeing too soon below the surface.
Although I hated you as you did me—
Later—I could do that for Agatha,
And did it; and the gold flowed—for a while.
I was across the ocean, trying wildly
Not to wish both of you and your new home
Were dead. You had taken everything from me,
And I might have some peace if one of you,
Or both of you, were gone. Call it the devil,
Or not, but that's what was alive in me
While I was over there where I was warned,
Early, of what was coming. I sold all mine
For someone else to lose, which is finance,
And somehow failed—I'll hardly say forgot—
To show you the same seasonable way
Out of that golden hole. I must have known
Down in me, and with all my talk of houses
Falling or standing upright in all weather,

Part Fifth

That I had thrown your world, and Agatha's,
Cruelly out of its course, and so far out
As never to return as the same world.
My only word to you from over there
Was an evasion and a temporizing,
Telling you nothing, offering you nothing
But a few shadowy promises. When you found
The truth, it was too hard for Agatha,
Who was not fit for shipwreck at that time;
For, as you said, all women are not made
Of iron entirely. I shall die not knowing
How near a madman I had then become,
Or whether there were devils. Tell yourself,
And let there be no doubt, that I destroyed her
While I believed I was destroying you.
It was too dark for me to see just then
What I was doing—for my only light
Was fire that was in me; and fire like that
Is fire that has no light. You hear me saying
That I did this, and that my first exploit
In Sharon, on returning, was to stand
At Agatha's grave and thank God she was there.
She was away from you, and as much mine
As yours—or my devouring self-defeat
Would so believe. I would go there at night
And talk to her. She was the only thing
I ever wanted that I could not have.
You took her from me, when she was almost . . .

The Glory of the Nightingales

Malory, if you care to open that drawer,
You will find in it the same implement
That you brought yesterday."

                                    Nightingale's voice
Was trembling for the second time that day,
And then was silent. Malory left his chair
And moved away again towards the window
That looked on those unceasing little waves
Which had no rest. They would have rest sometime,
And when they rested they would not be waves.
Should he be Malory when he was resting,
He thought, or only as much of earth and air
And water as there was of him to be moving
Again somewhere and to be something else.
He had almost forgotten Nightingale,
Who had said little to him that was new,
And nothing that was false. He had been false
Until it was no matter what else he was,
Or what he had to say, or what he did,
Said Malory; and that was easy saying
For one in whom even hate had now no home.

And was that all, and had he come in vain
So far to find where vengeance was not his?
Those flashing waves were life; they were not death,
Or sleep. The power that made them flash was power,
It was not nothing. It was like a wish

To live, and an awakening wish to serve.
It was not what he found in Agatha's
Untroubled smile or in her living eyes
Between him and her grave; it was, perhaps,
More like what he saw now while she was coming,
With the same eyes, and the same smile in them,
Between him and a sea that had no rest,
And for another moment while she flashed
And faded between him and Nightingale,
Whose eyes were those of a man trying to smile
Because he was to die.

                            "Never forget,
Malory," said his ruminating host,
"What an unvisualized and writhing city
Of pain and fear a million men and women
Would make, who are not well and have too long
To live, and strangely are not ready to die.
I don't know what a million men and women
Are worth to you, yet I can estimate,
Remotely, what equipment and resource
Is in them of indignant uselessness,
And misery too merciless and too harsh,
And undeserved, to be explainable
To eyes of earth. I have the eminence
Of my deserts, and therefore am exempt
From your attention. Now go for a walk,
Down by the shore, where you may find some shells

The Glory of the Nightingales

That once were filled with unaspiring life,
And leave me to inhabit my grand mansion,
Which I have always wanted, by the sea."

VI

WITH his word that he would stay until tomorrow,
    He obeyed; and with a willingness unknown
For so long that he was loth to recognize it
As a wish to breathe again the breath of life,
He could see, like fallen walls of an old city
In a plain where there was only sand and death,
Dead emptiness of hate and desolation
That he would not recall. He would forget it,
And by it be forgotten. He was tired
Of deserts, and had found at last that his,
Where he had groped and stumbled for so long,
Had been too barren a place even for death
To dwell in. Death had abandoned Malory,
Or was not yet his friend. There was no friend
Anywhere, and he saw no need of one.
If glimmerings that attended him today
Were intimations of a coming light,
He was to be alone for a long time,
And with no friends in sight. If he deserved them,
Or if his light required them in his picture,
No doubt they would be there eventually.
But for the present they were far away,
And better so. He would have little for them,
Or for the solace of their wakeful ears.
Their presence would be kindness at his heels,
And underfoot, imploring to be stepped on
If in the way, and angry if obeyed.

The Glory of the Nightingales

There was a time for friends that was not now.
If he should find a way back to himself,
His enemies, long pursued and long forsaken,
Would be his friends; for death, living in them,
Would be his life. There was no answer yet.
His fancies came and went, and were as vain
As a dumb wave that he saw burrowing
Among weed-muffled rocks to find a sound
That was not there. From where he stood, alone,
A few rocks and the sea was all there was
Of a life-burdened world except himself;
And he was not yet small enough to carry
A whole world's burden. There was hope in that,
If there was none in those recurrent waves
That came and lifted always the same weeds,
Until they were like coarse and floating hair
Of giant women drowned and turned to stone,
And fell to rise again to the same end
That was no end, and always came to nothing.
In clouds that came and went, there was at least
A sort of promise, for they came and went;
But here there was a promise of nothing else
Than waves and waves, and then waves, and more waves,
That went and came. There was nothing in them for men
Whose imminent need to live was a parole
And a probation; and there was less for men
Who came from Sharon yesterday to die.
He found an inland way among the trees

More to his fancy. They would not go from him
And then come back. He was tired of things that moved
And did no more. He had been one of them
So long, for the achievement of so little,
That he would rest—who had no power to rest.
He should not rest again until he died,
Which was a thing to know. If Nightingale
Told him of what was his, he would deny it,
And say it was not his. Nothing was his,
Which was another thing for him to know.

In the afternoon, with Nightingale before him,
Silent, in the same room, in the same chair,
Malory found the task of saying nothing
Only a somewhat easier one than speech.
Having his wits, he was uncomfortable
With Nightingale, who was aware of more
Than would have been a pleasure to explain
Of Malory's constraint. If in his eyes
There was a stricken willingness to smile,
With any encouragement, he could find none
In Malory's face, and said, indifferently,
"I'm glad you keep your word, and are to stay
With me until tomorrow. I like doctors,
Lawyers, and criminals, and all true men
Who keep their word; also those competent
Grand-nephews of Jehu who drive our cars.
If you are willing, we'll have one of them

The Glory of the Nightingales

Here now, and we'll go rolling. With two slaves
To put me in and take me out again,
I do a deal of rolling, and feel the world
Rolling away—though you may not believe it.
For why should you believe me, Malory,
Whatever I say? And yet, you may as well.
I'll say a little more while we are going,
And seeing the world the Lord has made so fair
For our defeats and victories. *Vae victis.*
Pronounce it as you think a noble Roman
Might once have uttered it, and say it twice.
I've an impatient and laborious ear
For listening while I ride, so you need say
Only those words, and say them to yourself.
We shall have time to scan familiar scenes
Again, and I shall not be long in saying
All I shall say."

     Nightingale's word was good,
And he was not long saying to Malory
As much as was required of him to hear,
And hear without reply. "I shall not know
What you are trying to do if you insist
On argument, or on immediate speech.
So, Malory, put yourself aside, and hold
Your scientific tongue. Imprison it
Behind your teeth and say it is a tiger—
A thing to do a fractious deal of harm

Part Sixth

If it goes wild. Besides, I have no ears,
And I am rather helpless in some ways.
Remember that; also conserve a thought
Of millions who have never heard of you
Or me, and of more millions who are coming.
So for God's sake be quiet, and admire
The outside of God's world, which is not bad.
Perhaps we may as well not go to Sharon
Today. Perhaps we may as well not go
Tomorrow. I shall go there, before long,
For there the Nightingales have always gone
When they have done their singing."

                                    Malory stood
Once more by the wide window, where he saw
Those tumbling and unceasing little waves
Until it seemed that he had seen them there
Since he was born; and they were not his waves.
Yet surely they were flashing with a language
That was important and inevitable;
There were too many of them to be dismissed
By one whose life was only a little more
Of time than one of theirs. If theirs were lost,
Why should not his be lost and be as nothing
In a more stormy and unsounded ocean
Than ever filled the valleys of a world
For men to weigh and measure? There was time
For living in himself and on himself,

[73]

The Glory of the Nightingales

Like a thought-eating worm, and dying of it
Unthought of, or for life larger than that,
Larger than self, and one that was not death.
There was avengingly not time for both;
And his was not the least of wavering lives
That had not stood when shaken. He was not
The least of summoned men who had served well,
And, having lost themselves in a great darkness,
Had not returned and were no longer sought
Among the missing, and no longer missed.
Had he returned? Was this the light again,
Or was a darkness worse than any other,
A darkness only felt, deceiving him?
He was not sure of anything since that ride,
Except that it was over, and that hours
Made days and years, and not so many of them
As there were waves.

               "Well, Malory, by my soul!"
Said Nightingale. "If I've a memory left
Of anything pleasant, and a right to say so,
That was a pleasant ride. You like my ocean
Better, perhaps; yet even if it were yours,
You would not wear a window out with watching
The same one thing, and always the same thing.
I am the watcher who can swear to that.
We've had a ride; and since you are still here,
The prisoner of your word, we'll have some drink—

Part Sixth

Which is forbidden. I shall not die of it.
If I should die just now, I should be going
A little too soon. You, a benign pursuer
Of hidden miseries, and of hidden means
To rid a more or less debatable race
Of their pernicious presence, are excused
From caring, or trying to care, whether I die
Tomorrow or today. There are more reasons
For your not caring than I'll reiterate;
There are more reasons than there may be days
For me to say them over and be sorry
For being as I have been. For a man with eyes
To see more surely what there was before him
Than eyes of the less fortunate may see,
I have not seen so well as men supposed,
And may be still supposing. Twice in my life
I have been blind; and that was a bad matter:
Once when I sank my judgment and your money
Into that most unhappy hole in the ground;
Once when I kicked my decency and honor
In after them. My purpose is to say
So clearly what I did that I shall never
Say it again. I'm sure you understand
Everything now, except that I should do it;
And sometime when you ask a streptococcus
Why it's a streptococcus, you may learn
All that I know of a dead Nightingale
That will not die. I'll say no more of devils,

But out of all this ruin, I'll save a few
Opinions and ideas for the small profit
Of having them. I have not seen the devil,
But I have seen sufficient of his work
Not to make light of him, or to invite him
Into my house again. The ruin I made
Is not all ruin, unless you make it so.
But if you ask why Agatha was chosen
To be the innocent means and sacrifice,
You will ask more than me before you know.
I shall not tell you. I am too blind for that.
I was not blind at first with Agatha —
I was almost . . . But what's the use of time,
If it will not be done when it's all gone?
We were not going back, but Agatha
Was calling me; and when she calls, I go —
And do not find her. There is little for me
To find, wherever I look. My blemishes
And evils now are mostly a sad trash
Of memory to be swept and blown away,
Or blown so as to leave you a clear path.
You and the world are in a partnership
Too large and too impersonal to include
A presence of sick hate. You owe yourself
To your unhappy millions in your city
Of cries and silences and suffering hope.
And there are many millions more to be,
And to be stricken. The world is not all pain,

But there is pain enough ahead of it,
And in it, to ensure the resurrection
Of you and your awakening faculties
For the few hours that we call years of life
That you may find remaining. There's a bell
Ringing, and not for you. We are not subtle
Today, Malory; there's hardly need of it.
I hope it's not another one come to kill me,
For you and Absalom, the Lord's appointed—
Who lived a while in heaven before he died,
And was a king of earth, having what he wanted—
Have so enriched me with an overplus
Of armament that I shall need no more
To scare my ghosts and enemies away,
If one day there should be too many of them.
I'll fancy rather it's a man of law—
This time; and it's as well for you to know him.
You are not fearing lawyers; not today.
Wherefore, we'll have him in. He's a good lawyer,
And does not know that I'm not a good man.
He knows too many others who are worse.
He has no knowledge of the lights I had
And could not follow; and if he knew of them,
And of the several ways where I've been lost,
Most likely he would not believe in them,
Having no time for visions or inventions.
Another day you may enlighten him
Somewhat, as you think best. When you are here,

The Glory of the Nightingales

You and your microbes, and your apparatus,
Your staff, your patients, and your God knows what,
You will know why it was this house was built.
A knowledge that was out of my possession
Till yesterday is a good knowledge now
For you, and who shall say how many more?
A pleasant home for microbes, I should call it,
Though it has never been a home for me."

The lawyer's entrance came to no long writing
Of a long story. It was all revealed
In words that held a latent increment
Larger than any estate. It was not land
And houses, and abundant maintenance,
That Malory found when he was given to read
The text of Nightingale's last composition,
But an imperious, fixed, and lonely way
Of life in service. There was no escape
From the long sentence of his usefulness.
He was a slave now in a city of pain,
A pullulating place that was all places,
And soon or late the last abode of man
Till his departure. There was no fear of joy
To be a stain on his inheritance,
Except the lonely joy of being alive
In a good servitude, and of not being
Obscurely and unintelligibly wasted.
Now he could say what Agatha may have meant,

Part Sixth

Between him and her grave, when she was there
To welcome him with an untroubled smile
On his dark road—one that would still be gray,
For him, and endless, if he found no light
For others. He was alone, and would remain so,
Until he found more light.

                " So much for that,"
Said Nightingale; and having signed his name,
He smiled at Malory and the man of law
With purpose and approval. "It's all done,"
He said, "and I've a planet off my shoulders.
I was tired of being Atlas; for my world,
Though it was no enormous one, was heavy.
And now that you two estimable agents
Of my deliverance are not unacquainted,
I should be glad if you would leave me here
A while to be alone, and not to talk.
Be sorry for an ominous example,
And let yourselves so live that you may not
Be living on wheels one day in a large house,
Alone—not even if you have always wanted
A large house by the sea. You will come back,
But I'll shake hands with you for your assistance,
And wish you a good ride. This is a day
For riding, and a good day for some thought
On my part. It is not like every day."

The Glory of the Nightingales

They left him smiling, and, as Malory knew,
In more pain than his body alone could feel.
They rode as easy strangers, having no food
For malice or mistrust. If one of them
Acknowledged inwardly a futile envy
Of such an unforeseen and unexplained
Cascade of shining fortune for another,
Nothing was to be done to a man's name
Written by him whose name was his to write.
They rode, and had but little to say of him,
Who, seemingly, had said everything for once
And all, and on a small array of paper.
For an hour they rode, in the late afternoon,
With trees and fields and houses on one side,
And with an ocean on the other, darker
As daylight faded, and with smaller waves
That had a slower motion as they rose
And broke more quietly now, and made less foam.
They told of a beginning of long silence
That night, and were somehow, for Malory,
Like toiling, weary people, who were soon
To have some rest before they toiled again,
And for a season were not to be waves.
Having each his personal fancy for companion,
They rode, saying what the old amenities
Required as best they might, and they came back;
And when they came to Nightingale's, they rolled
Quietly in on crushed blue stone to find

Part Sixth

A strange house not so quiet, and a stranger
Within that was invisible, and a shape
Of someone that was no one, still in his chair,
With Malory's pistol on the floor beside him.
What Malory once had called his only wealth
Had given him wealth to serve, and without waiting.
Nightingale had said nothing about waiting,
And Malory had known why.

                         Alone that evening
With all there was to see of Nightingale,
Lying at last unharassed and untorn,
Malory sat with fate, and gazed at it.
"Well, Nightingale, you are quiet enough now,"
He thought; "and you have earned now, in your way,
Or in another way that was not yours,
The privilege of a sleep—if you are sleeping.
You have bound me hand and foot, body and brain,
To service. I owe to Agatha, and to you,
All that I owe mankind. It's all an owing,
For me, and shall be one till I have paid
To man my sum of knowledge, which is little,
God knows, though not so little as I should be
For hiding it, or for throwing it away.
The light you could not follow is not mine,
Which is my light—a safer one for me,
No doubt, than if it threw a gleam too far
To show my steps. There is no grief in me

[81]

The Glory of the Nightingales

For your release, and there is no hate now
For Agatha's. If I could bring her back,
By calling her, to live and die again,
I should be silent; for I cannot know
The pain there was that was not hers to suffer,
Because she was not here. I cannot know,
For certain, that your way, dark as it was,
Was not the necessary way of life.
There was in yours at least a buried light
For time and man; and science, living in time,
May find at last a gleam nearer than yours,
For those who are not born to follow it
Before it has been found. There is, meanwhile,
A native light for others, but none born
Of penitence, or of man's fear to die.
Fear is not light, and you were never afraid.
You were blind, Nightingale, but never afraid;
And even when you were blind, you may have seen,
Darkly, where you were going, and where you are.
For where you are tonight, there was your place;
And your dark glass is broken."

                              He looked up
From Nightingale to see, against the wall,
Dimly, and on dim wheels, a dead man's chair
With no man in it. Here was the same room
Where fate was waiting for him yesterday—
With a presence now of death to make it empty,

And the difference of a day to make it his.
Here was a place where gold would buy no sorrow,
And the embellished rhetoric of regret
Would soon be words forgotten, and no more.
There was nothing left of Nightingale but silence,
And a cold weight of mystery that was man,
And was no longer man—as waves outside
Were cold and still, and were no longer waves.
There was nothing left for Malory but remembrance
Of the best that was behind him, and life struggling
In the darkness of a longer way before him
Than a way there was from anywhere to Sharon—
A darkness where his eyes were to be guided
By light that would be his, and Nightingale's.